My Book of Heavenly Ways

About the Artist

Deb Haas Abell lives with her husband and two children in a cozy home with a picket fence, nestled in a small town in Southern Indiana. She hopes this book will put you in touch with heavenly help and healing...and the angel in you!

About the Author

Molly Wigand lives in suburban Kansas City with her husband and three angelic sons. She's grateful to be able to share her inner angel's thoughts and feelings with you.

Text © 1998 by Molly Wigand
Art © 1998 by Deb Haas Abell
Published by One Caring Place
Abbey Press
St. Meinrad, Indiana 47577

All rights reserved.
No part of this book may be used or reproduced in any manner
without written permission of the publisher, except in the case
of brief quotations embodied in critical articles and reviews.

Library of Congress Catalog Number 98-72642

ISBN 0-87029-317-6

Printed in the United States of America

Serenity ~ and the Angel in You

One of God's most precious blessings is the gift of serenity—the peace of mind that comes from embracing ourselves and others as lovable human beings.

The wisdom in this book is offered to put you in touch with the angel in you, who will guide you on the path to serenity. Feel free to jot your thoughts and feelings on the write-on activity pages or, if you prefer, keep your reflections privately in your heart.

May this book help you to accept your angel's message: You are a wonderful and worthy child of God. Your journey to serenity begins right now with a commitment to finding and following your own unique path to wholeness and love.

It may seem that serenity is impossible in our hectic world. With the help of your inner angel, however, you can create peaceful moments in every day. Simply taking a deep breath, writing a friendly letter, or even cleaning a messy closet can be acts of quiet renewal.

HARMONY ♥ CHARITY ♥ GRACE ♥ GOODNESS

But Life Is Hard...

It can be hard to see our way toward serenity when problems demand our attention, or personal relationships are filled with conflict and pain. By accepting our daily challenges—whether enjoyable or unpleasant, menial or meaningful—we open our hearts to God's serenity.

Through prayer and meditation, your inner angel can help you discover blessings and joy within life's most difficult and troubling times.

Keep On Searching

♥ Think of the three most difficult situations in your life right now. List them here.

♥ What blessings might come from these troubling times?

♥ What blessings have already come?

If You're Happy and You Know It

There's an old saying that goes, "Most people are about as happy as they make up their minds to be." It's also true that most people are happier than they realize.

Your inner angel can help you to treasure the forgotten or overlooked blessings of your life. Appreciate the flight of geese to winter homes, the rhythm of a skipping stone, the warmth of a kitten curled in your lap, the smile of a stranger, the trust of a friend...and experience the gift of serenity.

SMILE
God Loves You!

God has promised to love us, no matter what. This simple truth should put a smile on every person's face. So why are our faces often set in expressions of anger, boredom, impatience, or anxiety?

You have a lot to be happy about, starting with the unfailing support of a loving God. Let your inner angel help you find your serenity smile.

Mirror, Mirror...

♥ Look in the mirror. What expression is on your face?

♥ Make yourself smile. Notice that a soft, serene smile relaxes your face and eases your tension.

♥ Make a promise to smile at least ten times today.

Remember... God loves you!

We encounter many crossroads in our life journeys. We look at our options, make decisions, and move forward. Second-guessing the decisions we made in the past creates anxiety and undermines serenity.

With your inner angel's guidance, believe that you are in the place you are right now because this is exactly where you are supposed to be.

Oh, You Kid!

Listening to a child's laughter shows that serenity comes naturally to kids. Unconstrained by the inhibitions of adulthood, these young human beings can teach grown-ups what it means to live and love in the present moment.

God's love and acceptance show clearly on the beaming face of a child. Your angel can help your childlike nature come out to play.

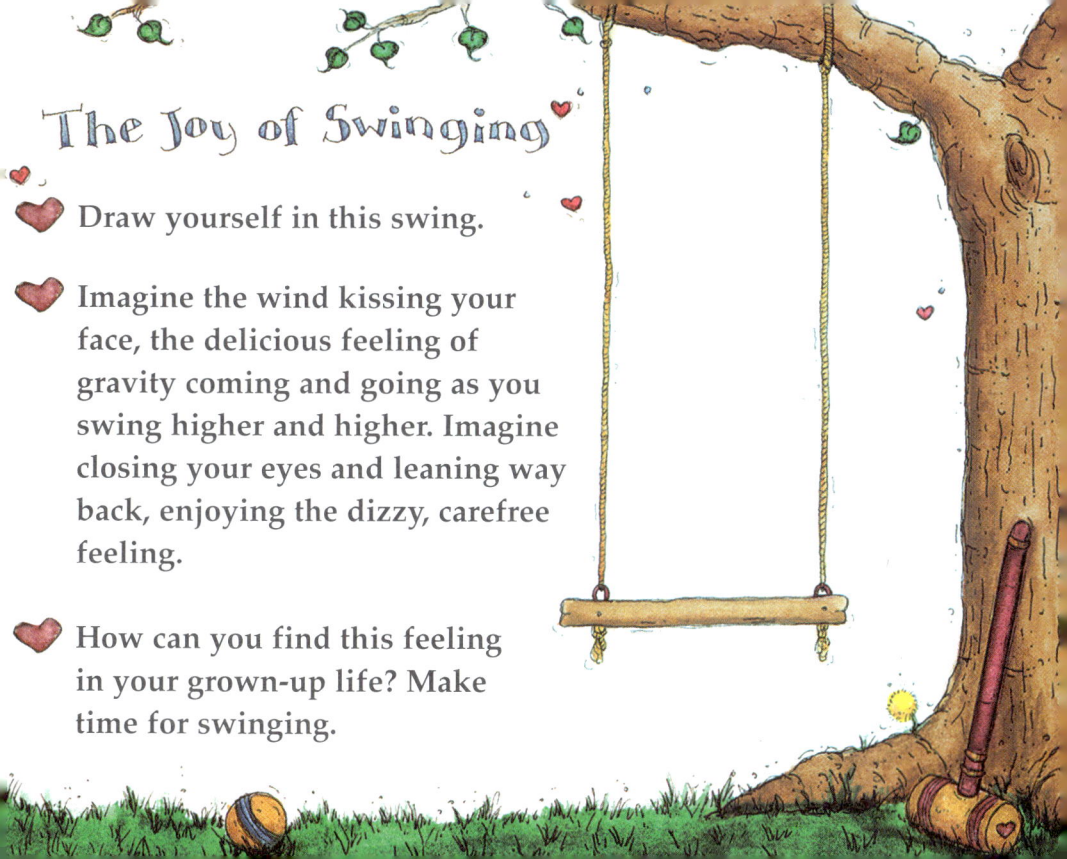

The Joy of Swinging

- Draw yourself in this swing.

- Imagine the wind kissing your face, the delicious feeling of gravity coming and going as you swing higher and higher. Imagine closing your eyes and leaning way back, enjoying the dizzy, carefree feeling.

- How can you find this feeling in your grown-up life? Make time for swinging.

Time Out for You and God!

The universe is filled with God's wisdom. God's power flows forth in the wind and rain. Divine beauty shines in flowers, birds, and clouds. Mystery fills starry nights. God's presence surrounds us always, but we must take time to be still and sense the serenity.

Ask your angel to find you a quiet, private spot in every day—a special corner of your world—where you can enjoy and appreciate life's little miracles.

In With the Good Air...

Many of us "forget to breathe" in our daily life. Yet focusing on breathing is a natural, restorative gift to ourselves. As we inhale and feel breath filling our bodies, we are reminded of the blessings we take in every day. Exhaling slowly, we feel our tensions dissipate. We experience calm, well-being, and a deep connection to all of life.

Let your inner angel help you become aware of the joy of breathing.

Breathing Journal

- Sit in a comfortable chair in a position you like. Describe your outer environment. Describe your internal feelings.

- Close your eyes and inhale slowly to the count of six. Then exhale to the count of six. Repeat several times, until you feel peaceful and relaxed. Slowly open your eyes.

- Does the room look different? Do you feel changed inside?

The Nature Connection

When we connect with nature, we learn much about living in harmony.

Sunshine keeps us warm, yet rain sustains our growing crops. Bees may sting, yet they make it possible for beautiful flowers to grow. Life's balance is apparent everywhere we look in nature.

God cares for every member of creation—from the lilies of the field to the tiny sparrows. By understanding that powerful love and passing it on to those around us, we rediscover the peace of serenity.

No Place Like Home

What a blessing it is to know the comfort of home—that special place in the world where you're accepted and embraced just the way you are.

Your "home" may be a physical structure, or a favorite spot in nature, or the feeling you get in the company of dear friends and family.

Invite your angel to join you on your homeward journeys. Ask your angel to help you bring a little bit of home into every moment of your life.

Happy to Be Here!

- Is it any wonder that one of the first things children learn to draw is a house or home?

- Draw your own "serenity home" right here. Include your special treasures, comfiest chairs, and dearest people. Use your favorite colors.

- Visit this page when it's not possible to be "at home" in person. Keep home always in your heart.

Heavenly Intuition

Hope

Serenity means having the confidence to make wise decisions about what path to follow. Some decisions come easily. But other times, after much thought and meditation, you realize that the logical thing to do is not necessarily the right thing to do.

Pay attention to all the feelings and instincts you have going for you. Prayer is answered in mysterious ways, and your intuitive feelings may reflect God's plan for you.

Rainbows

Each color of the rainbow has its own unique beauty. If all the bands of the rainbow were blue...or orange...or red, then it wouldn't be a rainbow anymore.

The same is true of serenity. It's foolish to compare your idea of serenity to your mother's or your best friend's or anyone else's. With your angel's help, you can discover your own personal serenity—the natural sense of peace and well-being that makes you glow with joy.

- On each band of this rainbow, write a phrase describing your personal ideas about serenity.
- Do you experience serenity every day? How can you get more serenity into your life?

Serenity + Courage + Wisdom

Do what needs to be done.

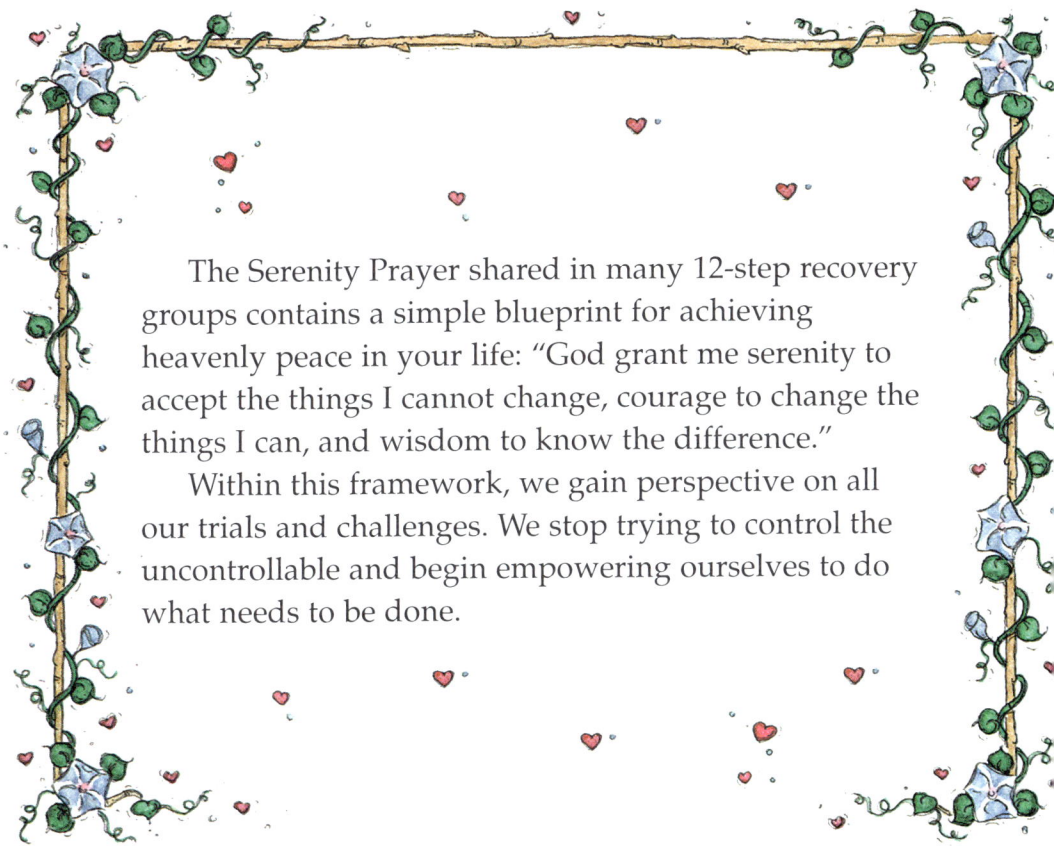

The Serenity Prayer shared in many 12-step recovery groups contains a simple blueprint for achieving heavenly peace in your life: "God grant me serenity to accept the things I cannot change, courage to change the things I can, and wisdom to know the difference."

Within this framework, we gain perspective on all our trials and challenges. We stop trying to control the uncontrollable and begin empowering ourselves to do what needs to be done.

The Optimism Habit

As you practice serenity, you'll find that you're able to remain positive even through obstacles and crises.

This doesn't mean that you'll be blind to the serious problems present in our times. Serenity allows you to do your best to change what you can—and then move from worry and discouragement to optimism and peace.

Your angel can help you see beyond the negative aspects of your world and your life, focusing instead on the beauty and blessings God has given you to enjoy.

I've Got Some Good News... and Some Good News

♥ Make a point of finding the good news around you today.

♥ In a newspaper or magazine, find two articles or pictures that made you smile. Use these happy stories to remind you of God's vigilance and care.

♥ Describe or paste your good news here.

Love Each Moment

Another challenge of serenity is to accept events as neither "good" nor "bad," but rather as the natural unfolding of God's plan. This acceptance frees us to forgive, heal, and grow. When we trust that God has our ultimate happiness in mind, we can let go of worry, bitterness, and resentment.

Ask for your angel's guidance to sort through the events of each day. Love and accept the mix of moments God has given you.

This Magic Moment

The only moment we actually have is the one we're experiencing right now. As you read that sentence, one moment ended and another began. See how fragile and fleeting each moment is?

Serenity means treasuring each second of life as though it is the last we'll ever experience. From this perspective, even traffic jams, arguments with your mother-in-law, or your teenager's booming music contain moments to cherish.

With your angel's help, learn to appreciate the small wonders in each moment.

Whistle While you Work

💗 Which household chore do you despise the most? Since you must spend precious time doing this terrible task, try to think of three positive things about it.

💗 Be grateful for having the time to do your daily work. Whether you're cleaning a closet, dusting knickknacks, or sorting socks, honor every moment of your day with gratitude and respect.

A Time for Everything, and Everything in Its Time

Have You Told Them Lately?

The Bible says, "To everything there is a season and a time to every purpose under heaven." But often, our human timetable doesn't seem to coincide with God's plan for our lives. When we ask God to help us with our jobs, our families, or our faith, we usually want a quick fix or easy answer.

Yet serenity and patience go hand in hand. Ask your inner angel to help you wait patiently and faithfully for God's guidance for your questions, doubts, and prayers. In time—God's time—the answers will come. Meanwhile, love the questions.

The Whole World in God's Hands

Serenity enables us to feel a kinship with everyone and everything in the world, to look for the best in everyone we meet. When we accept the biblical challenge to love our enemies and pray for those who hurt us, we bless not only those "difficult" people in our lives, but ourselves as well.

As your inner angel helps you to see the human goodness possessed by even those you have mistrusted or feared in the past, you'll begin to embrace each person as a member of God's family.

God Bless Us, Every One!

♥ Think of someone you find annoying or difficult.

♥ Surround this person with thoughts of love and understanding. Acknowledge that, like you, this "challenging" person is doing his or her best to live a good and fruitful life.

♥ Write a short prayer asking God to help you to accept and forgive the human frailties of the people around you.

Forgive yourself, too.

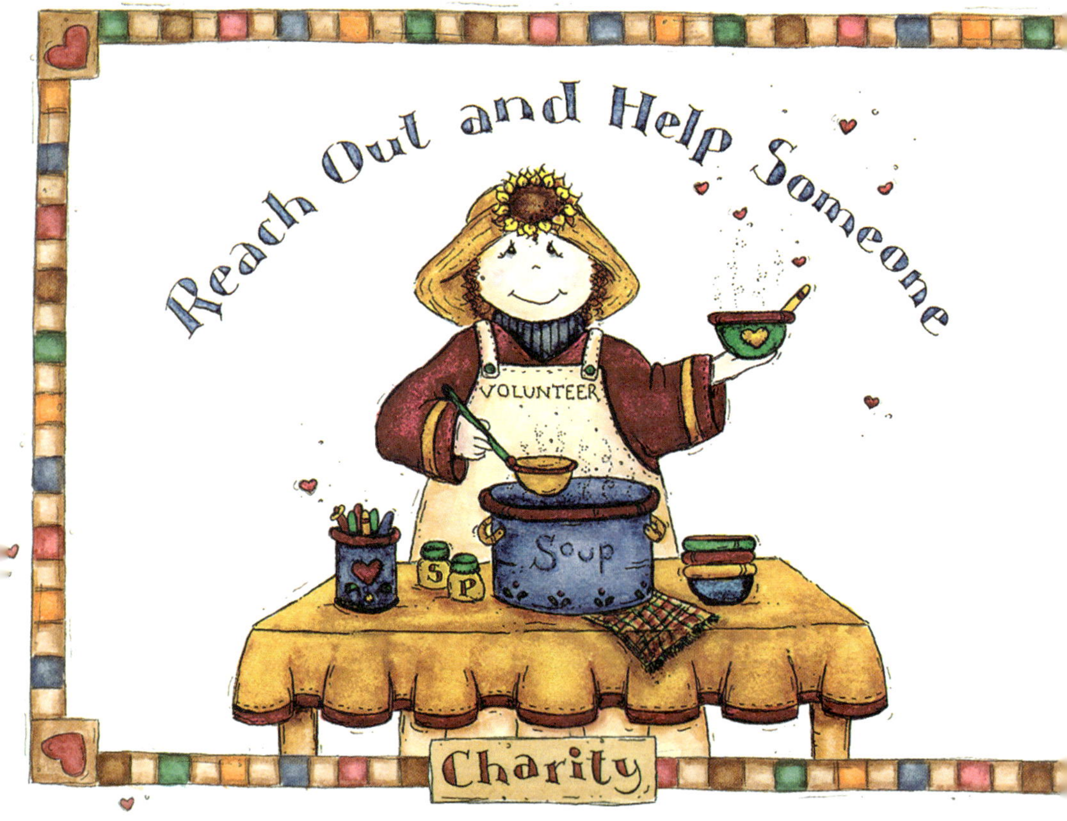
Reach Out and Help Someone
VOLUNTEER
Soup
S
P
Charity

Serenity comes more easily to those who give to others. By focusing outward on the needs and hurts of those around us, our own troubles are put in perspective.

As you explore your own path toward serenity, you'll discover the gifts you're meant to share with others. Not everyone is cut out for volunteering at a nursing home, or cleaning up a roadway, or sorting clothing at a homeless shelter. But each human being has something unique and valuable to offer. The pathway to serenity is illuminated each time you show kindness and compassion to another human being.

Little Actions, Big Rewards

We grow spiritually not only by committing to a specific charity or cause, but also by facing our daily journey with an attitude of generosity and grace.

Encouraging our children and their teachers, smiling at the bus driver, helping a stranger pick up dropped groceries—each act of kindness brings new smiles, warmth, and beauty into God's world.

Serenity allows you to approach every moment as an opportunity to do good and help others along the journey of life.

Reach Out and Calm Someone

♥ Is someone close to you feeling worried or fearful?

♥ Draw a picture of your troubled friend or family member. In the drawing, surround your loved one with beautiful flowers, colors, and other favorite things.

♥ Ask your inner angel to help you share your serenity.

Practice Makes Imperfect

Many messages in our world lead us to believe that we should be perfect—with thin bodies, great hair, well-mannered children, fat bankbooks, and success in everything we do.

Fortunately, God loves us just as we are. From Trappist monks to insecure suburbanites, from struggling adolescents to over-scheduled executives—all are equal and beloved in the eyes of God.

As we gain serenity, our inner angel helps us to accept imperfection and affirm the beauty and worth of all God's children—even ourselves.

God loves us just as we are.

Acceptance Is for Everyone... Even You!

God says we are to "love one another, as we love ourselves." Often, we take only the first half of that heavenly equation to heart. We are much more likely to overlook the mistakes of our friends and family members than to forgive ourselves for our shortcomings.

With your angel's help, treat yourself as gently as you would a treasured friend. Be your own patient, supportive companion as you grow in serenity and faith.

💗 What qualities do you think of when you're asked to describe yourself?

💗 On this artist's canvas, write your personality traits. Weave together words and pictures to depict yourself as a collage of beautiful humanity.

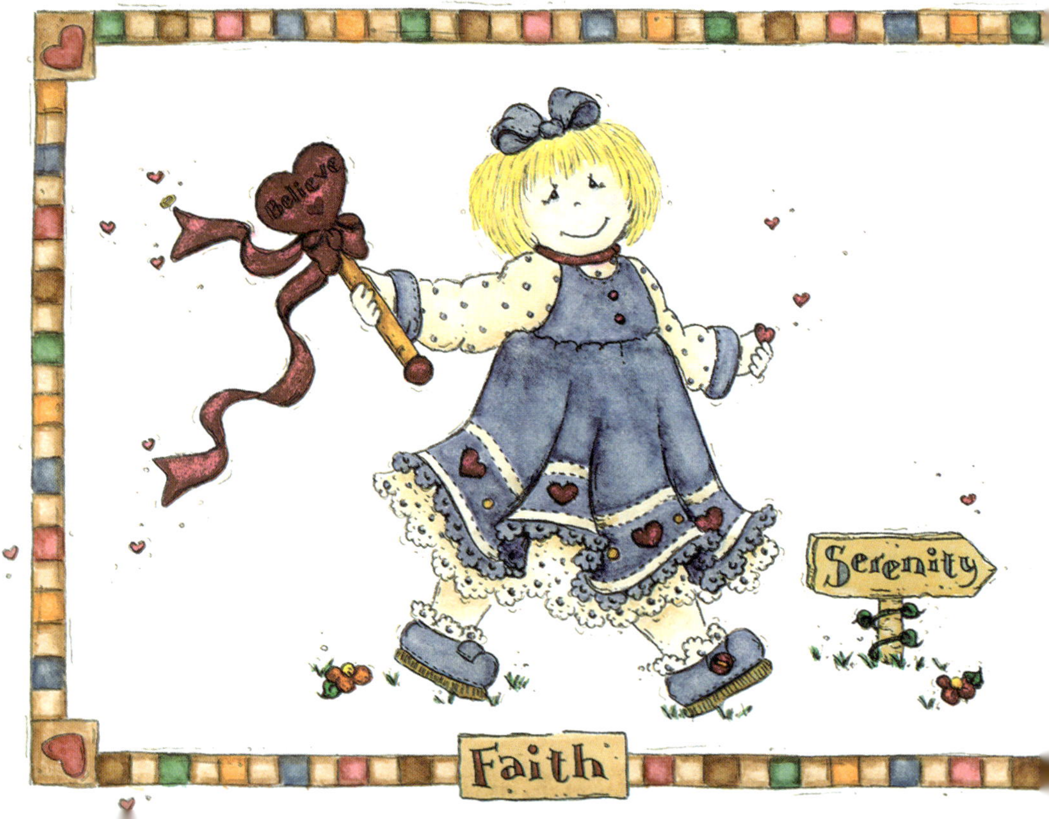
Believe
Serenity
Faith

Angel on Your Shoulder

When life gets hectic and demanding, we may lose our spiritual compass. The chaos of schedules, stresses, and demands seems to overpower the "still, small voice" of God.

But God's grace and love are with us even when we don't realize or appreciate them. Your inner angel is always at your side, ready when you are to help you resume your spiritual journey and rediscover the joy and peace of serenity.

Your Journey of Discovery

Let Faith Guide You

Serenity empowers you to discover your own path through life's trials and triumphs. Though you can't always see what lies around the next turn, faith in God allows you to proceed with confidence.

Even if God leads you to a different path altogether and asks you to abandon the trail you know, the serenity of faith will keep you looking ahead in acceptance while loving what's gone before.

♥ Chances are, your life's journey has taken many interesting twists and turns.

♥ Draw your spiritual path so far. With words or symbols, highlight the events that have shaped your serenity.

♥ Ask your inner angel for guidance at the crossroads still to come.

A Forever Kind of Hope

God's promise of eternal life is a powerful source of serenity and strength. If not for this wonderful promise, the death of a loved one or a serious illness would take away peace and happiness from even the most faith-filled person.

A beautiful world awaits us when we leave our earthly lives. Knowing this, we face each day of the future with hope and confidence.

A beautiful world awaits us.

You (and God) Can Handle It!

Serenity beckons us to believe God's promise: We won't be given any burden too heavy to bear.

Listen to your angel's message of reassurance: No matter what happens today or tomorrow or next week, your faith in the love of God will empower you to survive, learn, and grow.

All you have to do is ask, and heavenly grace is yours.

❤ Prayer is a two-way street. When we ask for heavenly guidance, we need to be receptive to God's response.

❤ Write a prayer asking God to renew your faith and guide your life.

❤ As your prayer is answered, write your feelings and insights here.

God's Listening... Are You?

A Gift From God
Believe
Hope
Harmony
Faith
God bless the Angel in You
Charity
Joy
Grace

Serenity is one of God's most precious gifts, a gift we can learn to nurture and cultivate in our lives. This book suggests some ways to find your own serenity.

The ideas in this book (or any book), however, may not always be enough to help you find the serenity you need at a specific moment.

Remember: God wants you to be happy. If anxiety, hurt, or regret threaten your spiritual reserves of peace and joy, seek the help of a friend, physician, clergyperson, or counselor.

Serenity Happens

Serenity can be a constant companion on our daily journey. By staying mindful of the world's goodness and beauty, embracing our own and others' humanity, believing God's promise of grace and love, and striving to savor each moment, we welcome serenity into our hearts.

♥ With your angel's help, complete these reminders about your path to serenity. Refer back to these insights when your spirits are low and you feel lost on your serenity journey.

♥ I trust in God to...

♥ I love people because...

♥ I appreciate this moment for...

Heavenly Peace for your Angel and You

About the Heavenly Ways Books

Once upon an idea, in a little heartland village, an artist named Deb Haas Abell toiled away with her paintbrush and paints. Inspired by the many angels in her own life, she created six heart-sprinkling characters: Faith, Hope, Charity, Joy, Harmony, and Grace. Their one mission in life was to spread the message that God gives each of us the ability to be an angel on earth...to touch lives, lighten hearts, and inspire souls.

These warmhearted spirits began to share their heavenly message through gift and greeting products in

Abbey Press's Angel in You collection. Before long, they were introduced to writer Molly Wigand, who translated their wisdom into books like this one—about Heavenly Ways to cope, even in the midst of life's hardships and heartaches.

But this is not just another pretty fairy tale. For Faith, Hope, Charity, Joy, Harmony, and Grace are present every day inside each one of us! May these books help you to discover your own inner angel...and may God bless the angel in you!

Heavenly Ways Books

Heavenly Ways to Handle Stress
Heavenly Ways to Heal From Grief and Loss
Heavenly Ways to Grow Closer as a Family
Heavenly Ways to Find Your Own Serenity

Available at your favorite bookstore or directly from:
One Caring Place, Abbey Press Publications,
St. Meinrad, IN 47577.
Phone orders: (800) 325-2511.